Houghton Mill, on the River Great Ouse, in Cambridgeshire.

Watermills

Martin Watts

Published by Shire Publications Ltd,
Midland House, West Way, Botley, Oxford OX2 0PH, UK.
(Website: www.shirebooks.co.uk)

Copyright © 2006 by Martin Watts.
First published 2006. Transferred to print on demand 2011.
Reprinted 2012.
Shire Library 457. ISBN 978 0 74780 654 7.
Martin Watts is hereby identified as the author of this work in
accordance with Section 77 of the Copyright, Designs and
Patents Act 1988.

British Library Cataloguing in Publication Data:
Watts, Martin
Watermills. – (Shire album; 457)
1. Watermills – Great Britain
2. Watermills – Great Britain – History
I. Title
621.2'1'0941
ISBN-10: 0 7478 0654 3.
ISBN-13: 978 0 7478 0654 7.

Cover: Daniel's Mill, Eardington, near Bridgnorth, Shropshire.
(Photograph courtesy of Eva Robinson)

ACKNOWLEDGEMENTS

In the preparation of this introduction to watermills, I am pleased to acknowledge the help of many people who have allowed me access to the mills in their care, and to all those with whom I have shared interest, enthusiasm and information, in particular Tim Booth, Alan Graham, John Harrison, John Langdon, Finlay Macleod, Bob Spain and Peter Stanier. I am particularly grateful to Alan Stoyel, who has willingly shared much useful information and his broad knowledge of watermills with me over a long period, and to Sue, my wife, for her interest, help and support throughout.

Illustrations are taken from material in the author's collection, including some drawings produced by him for English Heritage, the National Trust and Oxford University Press, to whom he is grateful for permission to reproduce them here. Other illustrations are acknowledged, with thanks, as follows: John Bedington, page 61; Ian Cartwright and Barry Cunliffe, Institute of Archaeology, Oxford, page 5; Mildred Cookson, page 59; Cadbury Lamb, page 63; Oxford Archaeology and CTRL (UK) Ltd, page 6; Robert Spain, page 4; Peter Stanier, cover; Alan Stoyel, pages 27 (top), 32 (bottom), 42 (top right), 57.

Printed in Great Britain by PrintOnDemand-Worldwide.com, Peterborough, UK.

Contents

The unusual Rowland's Mill, near Ilminster, Somerset, which dates from the seventeenth century. The domestic quarters were restored for holiday accommodation and the waterwheel and machinery repaired to working order in the late 1990s.

Historical background

The use of flowing and falling water to perform work by turning waterwheels was probably first adopted in the eastern Mediterranean region in the middle of the third century BC. The earliest description of a water-powered mill for grinding grain is found in *De Architectura*, written by the Roman engineer Vitruvius in about 25 BC, but the best evidence for early mills has been found by archaeological excavation. The first powered mills, turned by animals and waterwheels, appeared in Britain shortly after the arrival of the Roman army in AD 43. Although only a small number of watermill sites have been positively identified, many millstones that date from the Roman period have been found on a wide variety of sites and, as these are too large to have been turned manually, they are likely to have come from power-driven mills. In 1907 the stone foundations of a small watermill dating from the third century AD were excavated at Haltwhistle Burn Head, Northumberland, just to the south of Hadrian's Wall. The remains of a timber trough indicated where the waterwheel had been located and several millstone fragments were also recovered. The foundations of two timber-built watermills, dating from the second to the fourth centuries, were excavated at Ickham, Kent, on the course of the Little Stour river in the 1970s, and at Fullerton, Hampshire, the excavation of a Roman watermill site close

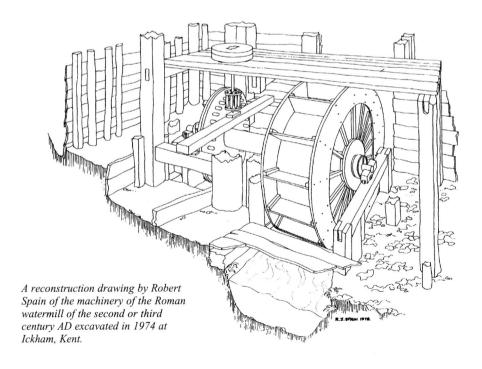

A reconstruction drawing by Robert Spain of the machinery of the Roman watermill of the second or third century AD excavated in 1974 at Ickham, Kent.

The archaeological excavation of a Roman watermill site at Fullerton, Hampshire, in 2001, looking south-east along the course of the leat, which ran from the bottom left. The four small post-holes indicate the position of a cill or sluice gate across the upstream end of the waterwheel channel. The two large holes on opposite sides of the wheel channel possibly indicate the positions of supports for the bearings at each end of the wheelshaft.

to a large crop-producing farm complex beside the River Anton revealed three phases of watermill activity, the last mill continuing in use into the fourth century. From reconstructions based on evidence found by archaeologists, it appears that a Roman watermill comprised a vertical waterwheel, usually undershot, which drove a single pair of millstones through right-angle gearing.

For the two centuries following the withdrawal of the Roman army in AD 410, no evidence has been found for the survival of such sophisticated machines as watermills, but by the eighth century they were again being built in the British Isles. In Ireland the remains of about a hundred small mills with horizontal waterwheels have been found, over one third of which have been dated to the early medieval period, many being built in the century or so after AD 770. In England the earliest evidence, both physical and documentary, comes from Kent, which suggests that watermills may have been reintroduced from mainland Europe sometime during the middle Saxon period. While the first historical reference is to a watermill at Chart, a share of which was given to the royal manor at Wye in AD 762, the remains of a timber-built watermill dating from the late seventh century were excavated at Ebbsfleet, near Northfleet, in 2002. Two timber flumes or pentroughs, which directed water on to the waterwheels, were found,

The remains of an Anglo-Saxon watermill at Ebbsfleet, Kent, excavated by Oxford Archaeology in 2002. Two timber pentroughs or flumes supplied water from the pond, at the bottom of the picture, to two horizontal waterwheels. Timbers from this site have been dated to the late seventh century.

as well as a paddle from a horizontal waterwheel and some millstone fragments. As with two of the earliest-dated Irish mill sites, at Little Island, County Cork, and Nendrum, on Strangford Lough, County Antrim, the mill at Ebbsfleet appears to have been worked by salt water. Water was impounded in a pond at high tide and released on to the waterwheels when the tide had ebbed enough to provide a difference in the level or head available.

From the ninth century documentary references to watermills occur more frequently and by the tenth century they appear to have been widespread. The timber sub-structure of a horizontal-wheeled mill dating from the mid ninth century was excavated at Tamworth, Staffordshire, in 1971 and on the north bank of the River Tyne at Corbridge, Northumberland, the foundations of a mill that is thought to date from the late Saxon period were identified in 1995. Two timber structures excavated at Worgret, Dorset, and Wellington, Herefordshire, which are closely similar to each other in size and date, are probably also the ground frames of horizontal-wheeled mills. While there is some evidence of ironworking connected to the mill site at Worgret, the majority of these early medieval mills were used for grinding corn. The mechanical simplicity of the horizontal-wheeled mill, in which the waterwheel and

The mechanical arrangement of a horizontal-wheeled mill. A is the waterwheel, B the pentrough, C the spindle connecting the wheel to the upper millstone (D). The sole tree (E) and lightening tree (F) allow the whole wheel and spindle assembly to be raised and lowered, to alter the gap between the millstones when grinding.

Watermill and church at Fisherton de la Mere, in the Wylye valley, Wiltshire. The proximity of a mill to other historic buildings, such as a church or a manor house, suggests an early origin for its establishment.

upper, rotating, millstone are connected directly by a vertical shaft or spindle, has been taken as an indication that such mills were the product of peasant culture, for maintenance and running costs were low and the output of a small pair of millstones, often not much larger than a hand quern, was relatively small. It is interesting to note, however, that some of the earliest mill sites where physical evidence has been found were connected with royal manors or large ecclesiastical estates.

Domesday Book, which was compiled for William I in 1086, records over six thousand mills in England and it is likely that there were others in existence at that time, particularly in areas beyond the limits of the survey. The large number of mills implies that there must have been skilled craftsmen – millwrights – who were capable of setting out watercourses and building waterwheels and machinery, but the lack of archaeological finds suggests that these early medieval mills were generally insubstantial structures, which have left little or no physical evidence. It is also likely that some later mills occupy Domesday sites and may have taken over the hydraulic systems established in late Saxon times. The argument as to whether Domesday mills had horizontal or vertical waterwheels cannot be resolved from the evidence available at present, although it has been suggested that some of the lower-value mills recorded in Domesday Book may have had horizontal wheels. However, the increasing amount of documentary information, both ecclesiastical and secular, which becomes available from the thirteenth century onwards, and the earliest illustrations of watermills in England, all indicate that by 1300 manorial watermills had vertical waterwheels. Although more costly to build and maintain, vertical-wheeled mills represented improved technology and, more importantly, increased output. During the Middle Ages a mill was an important source of manorial income, providing a service that many tenants were obliged to use, with a proportion of grain being taken by the miller as his toll, a payment in kind. The majority of watermills were used for producing meal and flour for making bread and also grinding malt for brewing, although from at least the late twelfth century water power was also used for fulling – thickening and finishing hand-woven woollen cloth – and metalworking.

Among the oldest surviving watermill buildings in Europe is that at the Cistercian abbey of Fountains, North Yorkshire, which has some

The downstream face of the medieval monastic watermill at Fountains Abbey, North Yorkshire, before restoration. Some of the stonework in the lower part of the wall dates from the twelfth century.

The restored mill pond and mill building at Fountains Abbey in 2001. The brick extension to the right houses a nineteenth-century waterwheel that powered a sawmill.

A medieval watermill depicted in stained glass in Thaxted church, Essex.

Right: Reconstruction of the working parts of a medieval corn mill, with an undershot wheel driving a single pair of millstones through cog and rung gearing.

Below: Pile's Mill, Selworthy, in west Somerset. The small mill building with its external overshot waterwheel is probably more typical of the form of a late medieval mill.

The jointed cruck truss inside the waterwheel gable of Pile's Mill in Somerset. The roof was formerly thatched.

stonework dating from the 1130s, although it was rebuilt and enlarged in the early fourteenth century. The mill survived the dissolution of the abbey because it was still in use; in 1540 it was referred to as two water corn mills under one roof. In the mid nineteenth century a sawmill was added and water power was last used at this historic site in the mid twentieth century for generating electricity. The mill at Fountains Abbey is an exceptional building, however, and it is likely that most manorial mills were smaller, less substantial structures, as shown in medieval illustrations. Some watermill buildings contain ancient fabric, but early standing mill buildings are now rare and most surviving machinery dates from no earlier than the mid eighteenth century. Pile's Mill, at Selworthy in west Somerset, is an interesting survival, the core of the building perhaps dating from

Below: The external appearance of Sheffield Mill, near Fletching in East Sussex, belies its late-sixteenth-century origins; the rebuilt brick pit wall and the position of the nineteenth-century iron waterwheel indicate some of the changes that have been made.

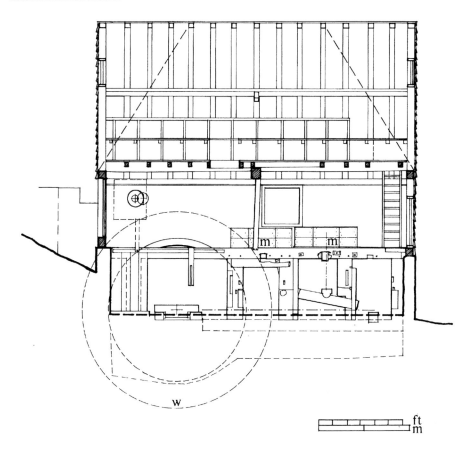

A section through Sheffield Mill, Fletching, East Sussex, showing the last working positions of the millstones (m) on a timber hurst frame that runs the length of the pit wall. Note the position of the present waterwheel (w) and the shape of the original hipped roof.

the late sixteenth century. It has a cruck truss roof structure and was originally a single-cell building of two bays, with an external overshot waterwheel at one end. The present machinery is of late-nineteenth-century date, but the external appearance of the building and its small size reflect its earlier origins. Of comparable size is the plan of Sheffield Mill in East Sussex, a small timber-framed corn mill which was newly built in 1578–80. Here two waterwheels were originally positioned along the side wall of the building, water being supplied by a large pond established to serve an iron furnace on the same site, which was operating in the mid sixteenth century.

A seventeenth-century watermill standing beside the fourteenth-century bridge over the River Welland at Duddington, Northamptonshire.

Siting and water supply

The construction of a watermill has an effect on its immediate surroundings, because of the need to control and impound water for use as and when required. The amount of flow and the height of the head or fall determine the power available and also dictate the type of waterwheel that can be used. Watermills were usually located with good access from well-used roads, and sometimes where a number of roads or tracks met. The concentration of water control at a mill site

Clapton Mill, Crewkerne, Somerset, showing two levels of water to feed one waterwheel. The main flow from the River Axe is taken around the brick wheelhouse and put on to the breast of the wheel, while a secondary supply, from a different source, is carried to the top of the wheel in an iron trough or launder.

Danby Mill, North Yorkshire, built on a new site in 1801. The raising of a dam across the River Esk, to provide a head of water for the waterwheel, caused considerable problems by flooding adjacent land.

often provided a suitable point for a ford or bridge, which was usually on the downstream side of the mill, where the water level was lower. Few waterwheels were driven directly by large rivers, most being fed by a more readily controlled flow of water taken off the main course of the stream. A natural rock outcrop or a weir or dam, built of timber or stone, across a river provided a fall and a means of diverting some of the natural flow into an artificial channel known as a leat or headrace. Many leats were taken off a

Below: The head of the leat at Sticklepath, Devon, just downstream from where a rock outcrop forms a natural weir across the River Taw. The difference between the levels of leat, left, and river, right, can be clearly seen.

A rubble stone weir across the Harbourne River in south Devon, with the leat serving Crowdy Mill taken off at the lower left. The leat entrance has been positioned to take advantage of direct flow on a natural bend in the course of the river.

A contour leat at Branscombe, Devon. The leat has been cut into the slope, the material dug out being used to form an embankment on the lower side. The gable end of Manor Mill is visible in the centre of the picture.

The mill pond at Kilcott Mill, Hawkesbury, Gloucestershire. The back wall of the mill is built into a dam constructed across the valley of the stream, a tributary of the River Little Avon.

Right: The large mill pond at Sheffield Mill, East Sussex. The pond was probably first established to supply water to power an iron furnace, which was working in the mid sixteenth century. Note the overflow channel in the left foreground.

natural bend in the course of a river so that water flowed directly into them, and some carried water a great distance to the required site and thus a great deal of time and effort was required for their construction. Their courses often followed contours and on sloping sites one side was cut into the hillside and the other embanked with the earth and stones that were dug out. Mill ponds are usually sited close above the mills they supply, allowing water to be stored until it is required for use. Clay was often used to make leats and ponds watertight, as well as to protect the timber foundations upon which some mills were built.

The headrace, with a weir to regulate water level and a sluice gate for draining down for maintenance and repair, upstream of Odstone Mill, Leicestershire.

The tidal pond, causeway and tide mill at Eling, Hampshire. The pond is filled at high tide and water released over the wheels inside the mill when the tide has ebbed enough to provide a working head of water.

Some mill ponds, such as those built to serve mills and ironworking sites in the Weald, are retained by substantial earthen dams, built across valleys, which also served to carry a track or roadway from one side of the valley to the other. Water levels are maintained by sluice gates and spillways so that excess water can be diverted in time of spate and the headrace or pond can be emptied for maintenance and cleaning. The principle of the tidal mill, which uses salt water impounded at high tide, has already been mentioned. After turning a waterwheel, the spent water usually runs away from the mill along a tailrace, flowing back into the river further downstream.

The proximity of mill sites sometimes led to disputes over water supply, for the upper mill on a watercourse could hold back the water from the lower mill, while water backed up to serve the lower mill could impede the waterwheel of that higher up, particularly if the

Below: The former tide mill at Thorrington, Essex. The tidal pond, now fed mainly by fresh water, is to the right of the causeway, with the tidal creek to the left.

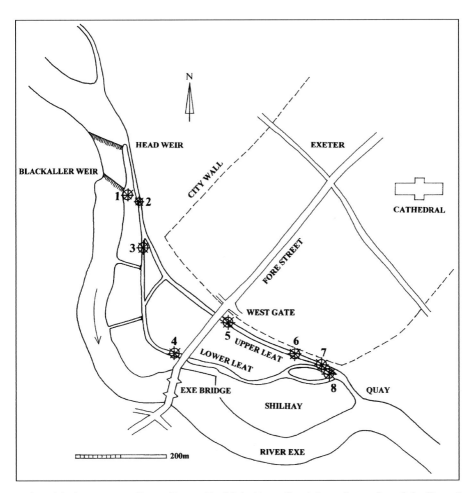

A plan of the leat system at Exeter, Devon. Established in medieval times, the two leats fed mills used for corn milling, fulling and other industrial purposes. From upstream to downstream, the principal sites were: 1, Head Mill; 2, Water Engine (which supplied the city with water); 3, Bonhay Mills; 4, Cuckingstool Mills; 5, City Mills; 6, Cricklepit Mills; 7 and 8, Lower Mills. By the eighteenth century the number and size of waterwheels were regulated at each site.

gradient was slight. There are examples of leats that served more than one mill, as well as leat and pond systems on rivers where mills were spaced at frequent intervals, each making use of a fall in the gradient of the river. At Exeter, Devon, where two leats supplied water to a number of mills serving several different industries, the number and width of the waterwheels that could be used at each site was closely regulated, to ensure that each mill had sufficient water. In the Sheffield area there was a particularly intensive use of water power from the late Middle Ages, the five main rivers and their tributaries providing about 30 miles (48 km) of watercourses on which over 115 mills, mostly for metalworking, were located.

A breastshot waterwheel driving a corn mill with a small overshot wheel installed by the last miller to generate electricity, at Melin Cochwillan, near Tal-y-bont, Conwy.

Types of waterwheel

The Romans used vertical waterwheels, that is, the wheel was mounted on a horizontal shaft and turned in a vertical plane. Vertical waterwheels are basically of three types, which are defined by the position in which the water acts on them: undershot, overshot and breastshot. While no physical remains have been found in Britain to show what Roman waterwheels looked like, the available evidence suggests that they were undershot, turned by the impulse of water

An undershot waterwheel at Cricklepit Mill, Exeter, Devon, installed in about 1860. Note the spillway gate alongside the wheel, for regulating the leat level.

The restored horizontal-wheeled mill at Siabost, Lewis, Western Isles. Water is carried to the wheel down the stone-lined lade and timber trough.

striking radial floats or paddles. The bottom part of an undershot wheel is usually contained in a close-fitting trough or wheelpit, so that the water can be directed on to the floats most effectively, usually by raising a sluice gate or penstock sited immediately upstream of the wheel.

While there is some evidence for the use of vertical undershot wheels in the Anglo-Saxon period, the mills excavated at Tamworth and Ebbsfleet both had horizontal wheels, with water directed on to their spoon- or scoop-shaped paddles through an inclined timber pentrough, a closed timber flume that tapers from inlet to outlet, to deliver the water under pressure on to the wheel. Standing remains of small mills with horizontal waterwheels fed by open troughs can still be found in more remote parts of Britain, such as the Northern and Western Isles of Scotland, where they continued to be used by crofters

The horizontal waterwheel at Siabost. Note the trough entering just to the right of the wheelshaft, and the sole tree and lightening tree.

Two of three horizontal-wheeled watermills on the same watercourse at Huxter, Walls and Sandness, Shetland.

Below left: An overshot waterwheel at work at Crowdy Mill, Harberton, Devon, water being directed into the buckets by a sluice at the end of a timber launder.

Below right: Overshot waterwheel and pentrough at Shepherd Wheel, on the River Porter in Sheffield, South Yorkshire.

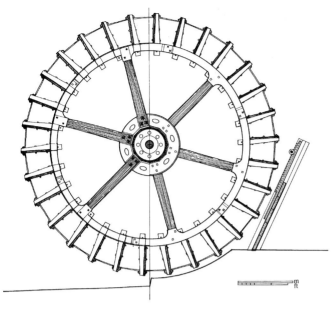

The undershot waterwheel at Cricklepit Mill, Exeter, Devon. The wheel is of timber and iron construction and was originally built to be carried on a timber wheelshaft. Note the angle of the penstock and the cill below the centre of the wheel.

and smallholders into modern times. They were particularly numerous on Shetland, where nearly a thousand sites have been identified.

An overshot wheel has compartments called buckets spaced at regular intervals around its circumference, which catch water falling on to it at the top, so turning the wheel by its weight. About one third of the buckets hold water at any one moment. Water is carried out over the top of the wheel in a trough or launder and the amount of flow is controlled by a sluice gate. In general terms, overshot waterwheels are two to three times more efficient than undershot wheels.

There are many intermediate heights at which water can be put on to a breastshot wheel, which makes use of both gravity, as with an overshot wheel, and impulse,

An iron breastshot wheel built by William Munden of Ringwood, Hampshire, at Alderholt Mill, Hampshire. The grille prevents any floating debris from entering the wheel.

A breastshot wheel fed from an iron trough
at Pontynys Mill, Longtown, Herefordshire.

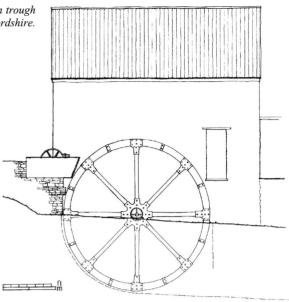

as with an undershot wheel. Low breastshot wheels, where the water enters the wheel below the level of the wheelshaft, usually have flat or curved floats, while high breastshot wheels have buckets.

From the middle of the eighteenth century the design of waterwheels was considered more scientifically, in order to make them more efficient and powerful, and high breastshot and pitchback waterwheels became more common. In both cases the breastwork immediately behind the wheel was usually built of stone or brick to a close-fitting curve, in order to keep the water acting on the wheel for as long as possible. A pitchback wheel has the advantage of the efficiency of an overshot wheel, water being put on

An all-iron high breastshot wheel which drove a corn mill at Knole, Long Sutton, Somerset. The wheel, which dates from the 1870s, was made by William Sparrow of Martock.

Twin iron pitchback wheels fed from an iron launder at Chase Mill, Bishop's Waltham, Hampshire. The wheels and launder were built by Armfields of Ringwood, millwrights and engineers.

A high breastshot wheel fed from an iron pentrough at Clifford, West Yorkshire. A bullock-hide screen attached to the wooden roller was rolled down to let water enter the buckets of the wheel through a series of cast-iron guide vanes.

at its top, but it turns in the opposite direction, so that the water leaves the bottom of the wheel in the direction of flow and thus does not impede its rotation. The design of the sluice or penstock by which water was let on to a wheel was also the subject of experiment and improvement, and a high breastshot wheel with water directed into its buckets through guide vanes, with the water feed being controlled by a finely adjustable sluice or hatch, was considered by some millwrights and engineers to be the ultimate design. In some cases, the hatch was in the form of a leather screen that was rolled down as the water level in the headrace fell, to allow the maximum head of water to be used at all times.

Improvements were also carried out to the design of undershot and low breastshot wheels, theoretically the least efficient types, to

An undershot waterwheel with curved iron floats, one of the improved designs introduced during the nineteenth century, in St Helen's Mill, Abingdon, Oxfordshire.

increase their power output. These improvements included the shape of the floats or paddles and the introduction of a cill immediately below the centre of the wheel, so that the water leaving the wheel did not impede the turning floats. The ultimate form was the all-iron wheel designed by the French engineer General J. V. Poncelet in 1825, although few waterwheels that incorporated all the details of his

Below left: Compass-arm timber undershot wheel at Cawsey Meethe Mill, King's Nympton, Devon, a rare survival that perhaps dates from the late eighteenth century.

Below right: A clasp-arm overshot wheel at Arden Mill, in the North York Moors. The simple nailed construction is similar to that of waterwheels dating from the fourteenth to the seventeenth centuries, remains of which have been found by archaeological excavation.

An overshot wheel under repair at Crowdy Mill, Harberton, Devon. The shaft and arms are of oak, the naves and shrouds of cast iron and the buckets of elm.

specific design were ever built in Britain.

Until the middle of the eighteenth century waterwheels were made largely of timber, usually oak, with iron fastenings and bearings. The life of timber wheels was relatively short, particularly with overshot wheels, which worked wet and had to carry the weight of the water that turned them. Because of this, the survival of early all-timber waterwheels is rare, but parts of several timber waterwheels dating from the fourteenth to the seventeenth centuries have

Below left: The iron waterwheel, 10.9 metres (36 feet) in diameter, at Daniel's Mill, near Bridgnorth, Shropshire, which was installed in the mid nineteenth century and is thought to have been built at Coalbrookdale. It is fed at two levels, high and mid breast.

Below right: A suspension-type waterwheel, built by Kirkland & Son of Mansfield and dated 1850, at Stainsby Mill, on the Hardwick Hall estate in Derbyshire.

been found during the excavation of mill sites used for ironworking in the Weald and Yorkshire. These remains show a consistency of design and construction that dominated until the last quarter of the eighteenth century, when cast iron was introduced into millwork.

With the increasing use of iron, those parts most vulnerable to decay were often replaced with castings; for example, cast-iron centres were fixed to a timber wheelshaft so that it was no longer necessary to mortise the arms through the shaft, which weakened it and allowed water to penetrate and cause decay. By 1800 some waterwheels were constructed entirely of iron, which allowed them to be larger, more powerful, more easily assembled from prefabricated components and longer lasting. Some early iron wheels basically translated the construction of a timber wheel into iron. However, a new design of wheel was developed in the early years of the nineteenth century; known as the suspension wheel, it used a lighter form of construction. The arms, which radiate from the shaft and support the rings or shrouds that carry the floats or buckets, became lightweight spokes, which were held in tension, rather than heavy timber or cast-iron arms, which were in compression. Adjustable cross-braces were necessary to keep the structure of the wheel parallel and true. Suspension wheels

The suspension wheel built by Robert Lee of Frome, Somerset, which was installed to drive machinery for spinning and weaving woollen cloth at Coldharbour, Uffculme, Devon, in 1821.

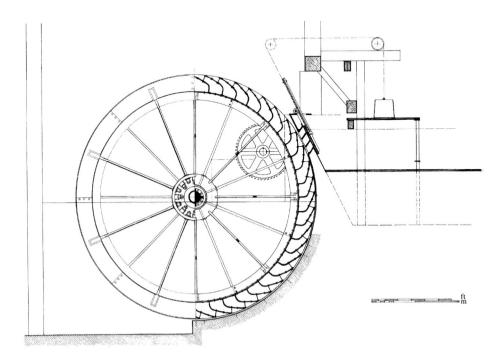

A Scotch mill, an early form of reaction water turbine, which was installed to drive the corn mill at Clun, Shropshire, in 1851.

were used particularly in textile mills, where large, powerful, low-maintenance wheels were required. Although many were built, few now survive; good examples may be seen at Coldharbour Mill, Uffculme, Devon, where a high breastshot wheel built by Robert Lee of Frome, Somerset, was installed to drive the machinery of a woollen mill in 1821, and at Quarry Bank Mill, Styal, Cheshire, where the last waterwheel designed and built by William Fairbairn in 1851 has been re-erected in the cotton mill.

At about the same time that General Poncelet was developing his efficient

An early water turbine made by Williamson Brothers of Kendal, Cumbria, in 1879, which drove saw-milling machinery in Gayle Mill, Hawes, North Yorkshire, a former cotton mill. A second turbine, installed in 1920, was used for electricity generation.

The top of the rotor of an Armfield 'British Empire' turbine, at Town Mill, Totnes, Devon. The vertical drive shaft carried a gear at its head, from which a drive was taken into the mill. When at work, the pit containing the turbine would be filled with water.

waterwheel, water turbines were also being developed in France by Benoît Fourneyron. A water turbine is simply a form of waterwheel that occupies a smaller space, runs at a higher speed and can work under a variety of different heads. Turbines can also work fully immersed in water and they produce comparatively more power than a conventional waterwheel, but they are vulnerable to clogging and fouling by leaves and branches. There are two principal types of turbine, reaction and impulse. In the former, water is introduced into the machine under pressure, turning a rotor as it leaves. In the latter, water is directed on to a wheel or rotor by one or more jets. Turbine rotors are usually fully enclosed in metal cases. The simplest form of reaction turbine is the so-called Scotch mill, which was introduced in the late 1830s. Other designs were developed in the United States and Ireland and from the 1870s many hundreds of turbines were fitted in British mills, often replacing waterwheels. Water turbines are still being installed in watermills, usually for electricity generation.

The brick building of White Mill, which stands beside the River Stour at Shapwick, Dorset, dates from 1776. It is effectively two mills, each served by a waterwheel in a central chamber. At one time both corn milling and fulling were carried out here. The mill cottage stands to the left of the headrace.

Mill buildings

The *Oxford English Dictionary* defines a mill specifically as a building fitted with machinery for grinding corn and, more broadly, as any machine or any building fitted with machinery for manufacturing processes. In a watermill the building and machinery are often inextricably linked, so that even when machinery has disappeared there are usually clues to its former layout and function. Because of changes in building materials, technology and use, watermills have a chequered history and, as has been noted, surviving machinery is unlikely to be earlier than the mid eighteenth century. As with any engine, parts wear and need to be replaced, and it is this process of continual change that makes mill buildings and their working parts of such interest. Many mill buildings occupy old sites, often rebuilt on or close to the footprint of an earlier structure, in order to make use of established water supply systems. There are numerous variations in the plans of watermills, much depending on where the waterwheel – or waterwheels, as many mills had more than one – were positioned and what function the mill served. The use of two or more waterwheels at some sites generally reflects the need to increase the capacity and output, for at the end of the Middle Ages there were

Two low breastshot wheels, each formerly serving a corn mill, at Church Minshull, Cheshire.

limitations both in the size of waterwheels constructed and in the machinery that they drove. In some instances more than one function, for example corn milling and fulling, were carried out on the same site, and the different processes were usually powered by separate waterwheels.

The demands of an increasing population and the use of water power for a variety of trades and industries from the early seventeenth century led to improvements in technology and larger mill buildings. Until the late eighteenth century most mill buildings followed local vernacular building traditions, with some interesting exceptions where they were deliberately designed and built to show some degree of architectural pretension, for example on large estates, such as Chatsworth, Derbyshire, where the mill was built with a classical façade facing the main drive to the house. The use of stone and, later,

The fine timber-framed and weatherboarded mill at Great Bardfield, on the River Pant, in Essex. Sadly the mill was virtually destroyed by fire in the 1990s.

The late-eighteenth-century estate corn mill in the park at Chatsworth, Derbyshire. The waterwheel was housed in the single-storey extension.

The upstream, roadside face of the tide mill at Beaulieu, Hampshire, a timber-framed and thatched mill which was rebuilt with brick walls and a tiled roof in the 1740s.

A late-eighteenth-century small country mill at Coleshill, Oxfordshire. The breastshot waterwheel, which drove two pairs of millstones and pumps for supplying water to the gardens of Coleshill House, is housed in the weatherboarded lean-to.

At Crowdy Mill, Harberton, Devon, the mill is built into the slope of the ground, and the millstone floor is accessible from a path alongside the leat. This feature may date from the time when customers each carried small amounts of grain to the mill and emptied them directly into the hopper over the millstones.

brick, for the construction of wheelpits and especially the pit wall, which separated the waterwheel from the machinery, was obviously important for stability and durability. The change of level required at a mill site, in order to provide a head of water, was also made use of, particularly in upland areas, where some corn mills were built into a natural slope in order to give access directly to the millstones from the outside, at a higher level.

From the mid eighteenth century corn-mill buildings became taller,

A late-nineteenth-century country water-mill at Lapford, Devon. The projecting white-painted feature is the lucam, which housed a hoist for lifting sacks of grain directly to the top floor for storage.

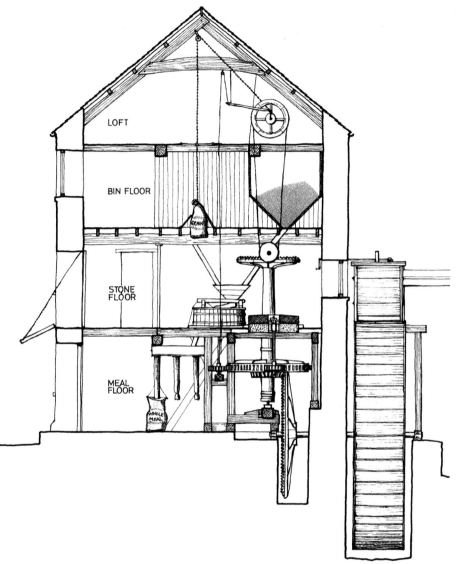

LOFT

BIN FLOOR

STONE FLOOR

MEAL FLOOR

A section through Morden Mill, on the Cotehele estate in east Cornwall. The layout of three or four floors is typical of many watermills that were built, or rebuilt, in the late eighteenth and nineteenth centuries.

with three or four floors becoming common, particularly in lowland Britain, where the trend was towards large trading mills with facilities for storing, cleaning, grinding and dressing wheat, to make fine flour. In upland regions mills tended to be smaller, with less storage room, and sometimes with additional milling equipment for processing grains such as barley and oats. A distinctive feature of upland corn mills is a kiln, with a floor on which grain was dried before it was

The fine double mill beside the River Till at Heatherslaw, Ford, Northumberland. The two mills, which were rebuilt on an older site in the 1820s, are virtually identical, each with a waterwheel driving three pairs of millstones and a pearl barley mill.

Below left: A pearl barley mill – a single vertical millstone that revolves in a perforated metal case to remove the husk and polish barley grains – in Longhill Mill, Urquhart, Moray.

Below right: The fan and dust cupboard that form a distinctive part of oatmeal-processing plant, in Felin Geri, near Newcastle Emlyn, Ceredigion.

An oatmeal mill and kiln, Longhill Mill, Urquhart, Moray. Note the distinctive revolving cowl on the kiln roof.

milled. Close to most watermills there are usually additional buildings, such as pigsties, stables and cart sheds and the miller's house, which form an integral part of the history and development of any site.

By the late eighteenth century there was great pressure on watermill

The drying kiln next to the doorway to the stone floor at Heron Mill, Beetham, Cumbria, with several redundant millstones leaning against the wall.

Above: The watermill at Monkoke-hampton, Devon, surrounded by ancillary buildings, including the miller's office in the foreground. One of the two overshot waterwheels, which still drives milling plant, is to the right of the building.

sites due to the demands of the textile and other growing industries, such as paper-making, and many mills changed use or were rebuilt, in order to make them more productive. Improved waterwheel designs and the increasing use of cast iron also had an effect on the design and construction of buildings and from the 1790s large textile mills were built using cast-iron columns and beams, in order to make the structure fireproof. Some

A brick-built corn mill with attached engine house at Caldewell Mill, Drakes Broughton, Worcestershire. The machinery was latterly driven by a Blackstone oil engine installed in the 1930s. The boiler came from a steam mill.

Langford Mill, Kingswood, Gloucestershire. There was a fulling mill on the site in the late eighteenth century, but this building, which dates from 1822, was a woollen mill, latterly used for silk production.

Right: Water-powered estate sawmill at Blair Drummond, Stirling. Part of the waterwheel can just be seen to the right of the building.

buildings used for purposes other than corn milling and textiles were less permanent structures, however, for example some sawmills and the buildings that housed machinery used for processing minerals and metals, which often have not survived or have been reused, although site evidence, in the form of watercourses and wheelpits, often remains.

Machinery and functions

There are several ways in which the power produced by waterwheels can be transmitted to perform work, much depending on the type of processing machinery that is driven. The majority of surviving watermills in Britain that retain machinery were used for grinding grain, for flour and for animal feedstuffs, although many industries once made use of water power.

CORN MILLING

In a corn mill with a horizontal wheel the drive is direct, with both the waterwheel and the upper millstone mounted on the same shaft or spindle. Where a vertical wheel is used, gearing is necessary to turn the vertical rotation of the waterwheel into the horizontal motion required by the millstones. Early mills worked with only a single pair of millstones, the upper stone being driven by a small gear, or pinion, from the pitwheel, a larger-diameter gear mounted on the wheelshaft. The difference in the diameters of the pitwheel and pinion also resulted in an increase in the rotational speed of the millstone. By the

Below left: The single pair of millstones driven directly by a horizontal waterwheel in the little mill at Siabost, Lewis, Western Isles.

Below right: The remains of Melin Castell Howell, Carmarthenshire. The layout, with a single pair of millstones on a hurst which was accessible only from ground-floor level, is a rare survival, reflecting medieval practice.

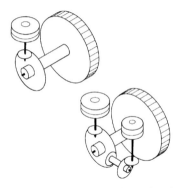

Above: Diagrammatic layout of a medieval mill, with a single pair of stones, and a treble mill, perhaps a late-sixteenth-century development that allowed a single wheel to drive two pairs of millstones.

Right: Layshaft drive at Shepshed Mill, Leicestershire. A horizontal iron shaft, driven by the pitwheel, carries bevel gears from which drives are taken to two pairs of millstones on the floor above.

end of the sixteenth century gearing was developed so that a waterwheel could drive more than one pair of millstones, the earliest recorded arrangement being the treble mill, in which one pair of stones was driven directly from the pitwheel and a second pair by a short horizontal shaft and a second pair of gears. Many different arrangements of gearing still survive, including the layshaft drive, which allows two or more pairs of millstones to be driven from a

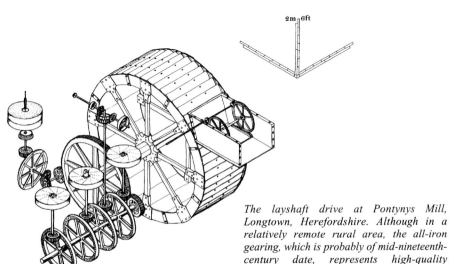

The layshaft drive at Pontynys Mill, Longtown, Herefordshire. Although in a relatively remote rural area, the all-iron gearing, which is probably of mid-nineteenth-century date, represents high-quality ironfounding and millwrighting practice.

Spurwheel drive, the most common gearing arrangement found in British corn mills.

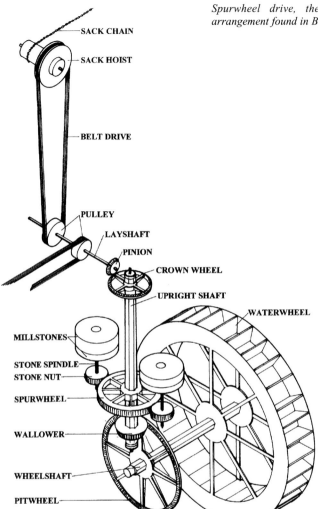

SACK CHAIN

SACK HOIST

BELT DRIVE

PULLEY

LAYSHAFT

PINION

CROWN WHEEL

UPRIGHT SHAFT

WATERWHEEL

MILLSTONES

STONE SPINDLE

STONE NUT

SPURWHEEL

WALLOWER

WHEELSHAFT

PITWHEEL

horizontal shaft. The most common gearing form found in British corn mills, however, is the spurwheel drive, in which a vertical shaft is driven by the pitwheel meshing with a small gear called the wallower. A large-diameter spurwheel is mounted on the vertical shaft above the wallower, from which drives to two or more pairs of millstones are taken by small pinions called stone nuts. In British watermills it is usual for the spurwheel to be positioned below the millstones, underdriven, although there are some interesting examples of mills where the spurwheel is above the stones, overdriven, an arrangement more commonly found in windmills.

The vertical shaft usually rises above the millstone positions to ceiling level, carrying another gear near its head, called a crown

Above left: A clasp-arm pitwheel with iron teeth meshing with a cast-iron wallower on a timber upright shaft in Tetford Mill, Lincolnshire.

Above right: The drive to the stones: cast-iron gears with wooden cogs in Middle Mill, Whitchurch, Pembrokeshire. Note the fork and jacking arrangement for raising the stone nut out of mesh with the spurwheel cogs.

Spurwheel drive to two pairs of millstones: the underdriven arrangement in Stretton Mill, Cheshire.

Above left: Overdriven millstones in Houghton Mill, Cambridgeshire.

Above right: The stone floor of Lapford Mill, Devon, with circular stone cases and secondary drives for the hoist, grain-cleaning and flour-dressing machines taken from a cast-iron crown wheel above the stones.

The stone floor of Mickle Trafford Mill, Cheshire. Note the octagonal cases – tuns or vats – enclosing the millstones and the large hoppers feeding them.

The sack hoist and fine bin loft in Venn Mill, Garford, Oxfordshire, which dates from about 1800.

wheel, from which lighter, faster secondary drives are taken by horizontal shafts. Using pulleys and ropes or belts, these power the sack hoist, for raising bags of grain through the mill, machines for cleaning grain and flour dressers, for separating fine white flour from the wholemeal produced by the millstones. As in the construction of waterwheels, cast iron was introduced for shafting and gearing during the second half of the eighteenth century, although wood continued to be used, particularly for individual cogs that were fitted into the working faces of iron gears.

FULLING MILLS

As well as using gearing, machinery can also be driven directly from a waterwheel shaft by the use of cams, stout projecting pegs that catch and lift hammers or stampers as the wheel rotates. Water-powered fulling mills were introduced into England in the twelfth century, using either vertical stampers or heavy timber hammers called stocks to full cloth. Bolts of newly woven cloth were put in a container with water and a scouring agent, then pounded by the falling action of the stocks or

A waterwheel driving a pair of fulling stocks; an early-seventeenth-century carving in the Tuckers' Hall, Exeter, Devon.

A pair of fulling stocks in Armley Mills, Leeds Industrial Museum, West Yorkshire. Here the ends of the stocks are lifted by tappets on the wheels in the foreground.

Below: A diagram showing a waterwheel driving a pair of fulling stocks.

stampers, which felted together the fibres and shrunk the cloth so that it was fit for use. Many fulling mills were built or converted from corn mills and they were widely distributed in the post-medieval period, but survivals are now rare. The best examples of water-powered fulling stocks are in the Esgair Moel mill, re-erected in the Museum of Welsh Life at St Fagans, Cardiff, and at Higher Mill, at Helmshore in Lancashire. Fulling or tucking mill sites can sometimes be traced on old maps from field names and from drawings which show the distinctive racks or tenter frames, on which the newly fulled or dyed cloth was stretched on tenterhooks to dry.

METALWORKING

Cams were also used in stamping mills, which crushed metallic ores for smelting, and to drive trip or tilt hammers for forging iron. It is possible that cams were used in the Roman period to drive hammers for working iron by water power, although the evidence is slight. Although once common, particularly in the south-west of England, the Weald, the Midlands and Yorkshire, few forge mills now survive. At

A forging hammer depicted on a date stone at Wortley Top Forge, South Yorkshire. Note the spring beam positioned over the top of the hammer.

The 1785 tilt forge at Abbeydale Hamlet, Sheffield, South Yorkshire. The tops of the two waterwheels that drive the hammers and the blowing engine, which supplies an air draught for the forge hearth, can just be seen above the wall to the right.

Right: The tilt forge, Abbeydale, Sheffield, showing some of the tools that were made there and the suspended seat on which the hammer man sat to work at the anvil. The steeling hammer in the foreground was used for forge-welding the iron and steel together, and the plating hammer beyond for shaping the tool blades.

Abbeydale, in Sheffield, two tilt hammers driven by a large-diameter high breastshot wheel have been preserved as part of an industrial hamlet where four waterwheels and many of the processes of working iron and steel can be seen. At Finch Foundry, on the northern edge of Dartmoor, near Okehampton, Devon, a small rural forge that once made shovels and edge tools (scythes, sickles and the like), three waterwheels are still at work and the smaller of two trip hammers is demonstrated from time to time. Like many other watermill sites, the buildings at Finch Foundry were formerly used for corn milling and textile production.

The overshot waterwheel fed from a header tank which drove the forge machinery at Churchill Forge, near Kidderminster, Worcestershire. The shears, left foreground, were driven from a crank on the outer end of the wheelshaft.

Coldharbour Mill, Uffculme, Devon: the woollen-mill complex looking along the headrace. The waterwheel is housed at the bottom of the brick tower, between the stone and brick building to the left and the gable end of the mill. A steam engine and the waterwheel were linked to drive the machinery in tandem.

TEXTILE MILLS

One of the main drawbacks of using waterwheels to drive machinery is their relatively slow rotation, particularly if they are of large diameter. The gearing used in corn mills generally increases the speed from say 6 to 10 revolutions per minute at the wheel to 80 to 120 revolutions at the millstones, and a certain amount of the power is also lost through friction between the gears and in the bearings. With the development of faster-running machinery for spinning and weaving wool and cotton during the eighteenth century, an increase in speed, as well as more power, was required and by the end of the century the ring gear had been developed. By fixing a ring of cogs or gear teeth around the circumference of a waterwheel, a large-diameter gearwheel was created, from which the drive was

The waterwheel at Coldharbour Mill, during restoration. The lightweight suspension structure can be seen and also the ring gear and pinion on the far side. Note the close-fitting curved stone breastwork behind and beneath the wheel.

Whitchurch Silk Mill, on the River Test in Hampshire. The waterwheel is housed in the lean-to on the right. The bell turret and clock are dated 1815, when they were put up to celebrate the Battle of Waterloo.

taken by a small pinion, so that the first driven shaft turned more quickly. In textile mills the individual machines for preparing the fibres, spinning the yarn and weaving it into cloth were usually driven by belts from pulleys on horizontal shafts that ran the length of each floor. Because of the demands of factory production, waterwheels had to work longer hours than before and auxiliary power was introduced in the form of steam engines. Where water power did continue in use into the later nineteenth century, water turbines often superseded waterwheels. Although few large textile mills still retain their original machinery, some have been turned into working museums where the sounds and atmosphere of a working spinning or weaving mill can be experienced. In addition to the mill, usually with an internal waterwheel or wheels, there are often important ancillary buildings such as engine houses, weaving sheds, cloth-drying stoves and the houses both of the managers and of the workers.

An iron low breastshot waterwheel driving a set of Bramah pumps in a small pumphouse adjacent to the combined windmill and watermill at Little Cressingham, Norfolk, which dates from 1821. The pumps supplied water for gardens and fishponds.

Edge runner stones outside a former paper mill at Stoke Canon, Devon, one of several located on the River Culm.

OTHER USES

There were many other industries and craft processes that made use of water power, which could be used to drive machinery by a variety of means, including cranks, gears and pulleys, these last transmitting energy through ropes or belts. Cranks gave a reciprocating motion useful for pumping water, for example in mining and quarrying, and for domestic or village water supply. Water power was widely used in

Flint-grinding mills at Cheddleton, Staffordshire. The south mill, left, was converted from corn milling to flint grinding.

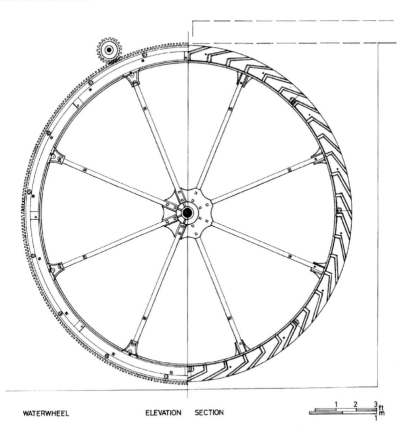

WATERWHEEL ELEVATION SECTION

An overshot waterwheel that drove a small pair of millstones, a threshing machine and other farm machinery at Umberleigh Barton, Devon. The drive was taken from the waterwheel by a ring gear around its circumference. The installation probably dates from the 1880s.

the mining and extractive industries before the introduction of steam in the eighteenth century, with waterwheels lifting materials and men, pumping water and driving stamps and other machinery for processing raw materials. As well as horizontal millstones, vertical stones known as edge runners were also used, to crush rather than to grind raw materials, for example in the gunpowder and paper industries and for making dyestuffs for textiles. In Staffordshire some mills survive that were used for grinding raw materials, such as flint, to make glazes for the pottery industry. From the early nineteenth century the ring gear also found favour with millwrights setting up waterwheels to power farm machinery, such as threshing machines and chaff cutters, which, like textile machinery, required lighter, faster drives. The remains of many farm wheels can still be found, particularly in the West Country, and, in common with many other uses of water power, there is still much study, recording and conservation work to be done.

The stone floor of Drewett's Mill, Box, Wiltshire, photographed when the mill was at work, grinding animal feed, in the 1970s.

Conservation

The production of flour was taken over by large purpose-built roller mills towards the end of the nineteenth century, although many watermills continued in use into the twentieth century, grinding animal feedstuffs. The mill conservation movement began in the 1890s with the preservation of a small number of windmills as landmarks, but the conservation of watermills was slow to gain momentum by comparison. In the early years of the twentieth century one of the small, horizontal-wheeled mills on Shetland was restored, for antiquarian interest, but it was not until the early 1930s that one of the first watermills to be preserved, at Shalford, near Guildford in Surrey, was acquired by a group of unconventional conservationists known as Ferguson's Gang and presented to the National Trust. In 1946, after many mills had closed down and some had been stripped of their machinery during the Second World War, the Windmill Section of the Society for the Protection of

The atmosphere of a working mill; the meal floor of Maxey Mill, Cambridgeshire, with two pairs of stones grinding barley for pig feed.

Shalford Mill, Surrey, one of the first watermills to be preserved and taken on by the National Trust.

Ancient Buildings, which was formed in 1931, extended its brief to include watermills.

Some watermills remained in use into the second half of the twentieth century and, as they have always outnumbered windmills in Britain, the threat to their longer-term survival was perhaps not so obvious. While much of the water-powered machinery that was built to provide for the needs of people, in terms of flour and meal, textiles, tools and other essential products, has now disappeared, many mill buildings survive. Many watermills still retain waterwheels, turbines and other machinery and some are open to the public. A small number still produce wholemeal flour, using traditional horizontal millstones, and some textile mills still work, producing woollen cloth. While the domestic scale and picturesque locations of many watermills have made them prime targets for conversion to other uses, particularly houses, some sites are finding a new purpose as producers of green energy, keeping alive the watercourses and hydraulic systems that, in some cases, may have been in use for over a millennium.

The Town Mill at Lyme Regis, Dorset, showing the front of the mill house and the new bakery in the former cart house.

Glossary

Bearing: the static part of a machine in which a journal runs.

Beetling mill: a mill in which linen cloth was pounded to produce a sheen.

Breastshot wheel: a vertical waterwheel where the water enters at about the level of the wheelshaft, driven by both the impulse and the weight of the water.

Cam: a projection on a wheel or shaft to transmit movement to another part of the machinery.

Clasp arm: a form of construction used for waterwheels and gear wheels where two pairs of arms form a square at the centre that boxes the shaft on to which the wheel is fixed.

Cog: an individual timber tooth inserted into a gearwheel.

Compass arm: a form of construction in which the arms of a waterwheel or gear are mortised through the shaft.

Crown wheel: a horizontal-face gear, with its cogs or teeth usually projecting upwards, from which drives are taken by pinions and layshafts.

Double mill: a mill that contains two sets of machinery or millstones, often driven by separate waterwheels.

Dressing: the art of preparing the working faces of millstones for grinding. Also used for sieving meal to make a finer flour.

Edge runner stones: a pair of vertically mounted stones that rotate on a fixed horizontal bedstone, used for crushing rather than grinding.

Eye: the hole through the centre of a millstone.

Fulling mill: a mill in which woven cloth is scoured and beaten to felt the fibres together. Also known as a 'tucking' or 'walk' mill.

Grindstone: a single, vertically mounted rotating stone used for sharpening tools.

Harps: a pattern of furrows laid out in triangular segments on a millstone.

Horizontal wheel: a waterwheel that rotates in a horizontal plane.

Hurst: the sturdy timber frame that supports the millstones in a corn mill or the hammers in a forge mill.

Impulse turbine: a form of water turbine in which jets of water are directed on to a rotor.

Journal: circular part of a shaft, usually of metal, which runs in a bearing.

Lade: a Scottish term for a man-made millstream. (See *Leat*.)

Lantern pinion: a driven gear formed of two discs with staves between which serve as cogs.

Launder: a trough, usually of timber, that leads water on to a waterwheel.

Layshaft drive: a gearing layout in which the drive is transmitted by horizontal shafting and face or bevel gearing.

Leat: a man-made stream that brings water to a waterwheel or mill, called *lade* in Scotland and *goit* in Yorkshire.

Meal: the product of grinding grain between millstones.

Millstone: one of a pair of usually horizontal stones for grinding corn.

Millwright: traditionally, someone who builds and maintains mills.

Naves: the iron centres fixed to a wheelshaft from which the arms radiate.

Overdriven: machinery, particularly millstones, driven from above.

Overshot wheel: a waterwheel driven by water entering at the top and turning it by the weight of the water in its buckets.

Penstock: a sluice or hatch that regulates the flow of water on to a waterwheel or turbine.

Pinion: the smaller wheel of two wheels in gear, and driven by the larger wheel. Sometimes referred to as a *nut*.

Pitchback wheel: a waterwheel in which water enters at the top but turns the wheel backwards, in the opposite direction to an overshot wheel.

Pitwheel: the primary driven gear in a watermill, usually fixed to the wheelshaft, with its lower half turning in a pit.

Quern: a pair of small diameter millstones, turned by hand, usually for grinding grain.

Race: a channel bringing water to or from a millwheel.

Reaction turbine: a form of water turbine in which all the water passages are filled and the rotor is turned by the energy stored in the water as it passes through the machine.

The eighteenth-century Mill Green Mill, astride the River Lea, at Hatfield, Hertfordshire.

Roller mill: a machine with cylindrical rollers for crushing grain or other raw materials. Also a type of mill developed during the nineteenth century in which a series of rolls in combination with sieves is used to produce fine flour.

Runner: the moving stone of a pair of millstones. Also a block of stone used in a grinding pan for reducing flints, etc, for making pottery glazes.

Rynd: an iron fitting on which the upper, moving millstone is hung.

Scotch mill: a reaction turbine with S-shaped arms patented in 1839.

Sliding hatch: a form of waterwheel penstock in which the gate is depressed so that water is fed on to a wheel over its top, thus utilising a better head.

Spindle: a small-diameter shaft, usually of iron.

Spurwheel drive: a gearing form in which a number of drives can be taken off the periphery of a spur gear. In a corn mill the spurwheel is usually horizontal and a number of pairs of millstones can be grouped around a central shaft.

Stampers: vertical timbers, sometimes shod with iron, raised by cams and used to break up or press raw materials.

Stocks: wooden hammers in a fulling mill for beating cloth to scour it.

Suspension wheel: a form of iron waterwheel in which heavy timber or iron arms are replaced by lightweight iron rods and cross-braces that hold the structure in tension.

Tenter frame: a timber framework with rows of small metal hooks on which cloth is spread to dry and shrink after fulling or dyeing.

Threshing machine: a farm machine used for separating grain from straw and chaff after harvesting.

Tide mill: a watermill worked by salt water that has been impounded at high tide and is released on to a waterwheel or wheels as the tide falls.

Treble mill: a watermill in which two sets of millstones are driven by a single waterwheel, one set directly, the second set by an additional pair of gears.

Tucking: a West Country term for fulling.

Underdriven: machinery, particularly millstones, driven from below.

Undershot wheel: a waterwheel driven by the impulse of water striking the floats at or near the bottom of the wheel.

Vertical waterwheel: a waterwheel that rotates in a vertical plane.

Wallower: the first gear driven by the pitwheel in a watermill.

Water turbine: a developed form of waterwheel that can be fully immersed in water and work more efficiently, providing more power under a variety of heads.

Wheelshaft: the main horizontal drive shaft in a watermill, on which a waterwheel is mounted.

Further reading

British watermills have not received the same depth of study as windmills, although the balance has been redressed somewhat in recent years. For general historical and technical background, the following publications provide a good overview:

Holt, Richard. *The Mills of Medieval England.* Blackwell Publishing, 1988.
Langdon, John. *Mills in the Medieval Economy.* Oxford University Press, 2004.
Reynolds, John. *Watermills and Windmills.* Evelyn, 1970.
Reynolds, Terry S. *Stronger than a Hundred Men, A History of the Vertical Water Wheel.* Johns Hopkins University Press, 1983.
Watts, Martin. *Water and Wind Power.* Shire, 2000; reprinted 2005.
Watts, Martin. *The Archaeology of Mills and Milling.* Tempus, 2002.
Wikander, Örjan (editor). *Handbook of Ancient Water Technology.* Brill, 2000.

There are a number of local, regional and county studies and some more detailed studies of individual mills and specific industries, a representative selection being:

Allison, K. J. *East Riding Water-Mills.* East Yorkshire Local History Society, 1970.
Ball, Christine, Crossley, David and Flavell, Neville. *Water Power on the Sheffield Rivers.* Sheffield, 2006.
Benham, Hervey. *Some Essex Water Mills.* Mersea Bookshop, 1983.
Bonson, Tony. *Driven by the Dane. Nine Centuries of Waterpower in South Cheshire and North Staffordshire.* Midland Wind and Water Mills Group, 2003.
Booth, D. T. N. *Warwickshire Watermills.* Midland Wind and Watermills Group, 1978.
Cleere, Henry, and Crossley, David. *The Iron Industry of the Weald.* Merton Priory Press, 1995.
Foreman, Wilfred. *Oxfordshire Mills.* Phillimore, 1983.
Graham, Alan; Draper, Jo; and Watts, Martin. *The Town Mill, Lyme Regis, Archaeology and History AD 1340–2000.* The Town Mill Trust, 2005.
Harrison, John K. *Eight Centuries of Milling in North East Yorkshire.* North York Moors National Park Authority, 2008.
Palmer, Marilyn, and Neaverson, Peter. *The Textile Industry of South-West England.* Tempus, 2005.
Rogers, Kenneth. *Wiltshire and Somerset Woollen Mills.* Pasold, 1976.
Shaw, John. *Water Power in Scotland 1550–1870.* John Donald, 1984.
Stidder, Derek, and Smith, Colin. *Watermills of Sussex.* Volume 1, Baron, 1997. Volume 2, Pheasant, 2001.
Tann, Jennifer. *Gloucestershire Woollen Mills.* David & Charles, 1967.

Information concerning watermills used for a variety of purposes can be found in local history and archaeology society journals and the newsletters and journals of the local and regional mill groups that now cover many parts of England and Wales. Details of these groups and other activities concerned with the study, preservation and maintenance of Britain's milling heritage can be obtained from The Mills Section, Society for the Protection of Ancient Buildings, 37 Spital Square, London E1 6DY (telephone 020 7456 0909; website: www.spab.org.uk). A valuable resource with a growing body of information and pictures of watermills, some of which is available online, is The Mills Archive, Watlington House, 44 Watlington Street, Reading RG1 4RJ; website: www.millsarchive.com

Watermills to visit

-The following watermills and water-powered sites are generally accessible to the public, although it is advisable to check opening arrangements in advance, particularly if travelling some distance. Other watermills and sites may be found which are open on a less regular basis and for special events, such as National Mills Weekend, which is usually held in early May each year.

Bedfordshire
Bromham Mill, Bridge End, Bromham, Bedford MK43 8LP.
   Telephone: 01234 824330. Website: www.bedfordshire.gov.uk
Stotfold Mill, Mill Lane, Stotfold SG5 4NU.
   Telephone: 01462 734541. Website: www.stotfoldmill.com

Buckinghamshire
Ford End Mill, Ivinghoe. Telephone: 01442 825421. Website: www.fordendwatermill.co.uk
Pann Mill, The Rye, High Wycombe.
   Telephone: 01494 472981. Website: www.pannmill.org.uk

Cambridgeshire
Hinxton Mill, Mill Lane, Hinxton.
   Telephone: 01223 243830. Website: www.cpswandlebury.org
Houghton Mill, Houghton, Huntingdon PE28 2AZ.
   Telephone: 01480 301494. Website: www.nationaltrust.org.uk
Lode Mill, Anglesey Abbey, Quy Road, Lode, Cambridge CB5 9EJ.
   Telephone: 01223 810080. Website: www.nationaltrust.org.uk
Sacrewell Mill, Thornhaugh, Peterborough.
   Telephone: 01780 782254. Website: www.sacrewell.org.uk

Cheshire
Dunham Massey Sawmill, Dunham Massey,
   Altrincham WA14 4SJ.
   Telephone: 0161 941 1025.
   Website: www.nationaltrust.org.uk
Nether Alderley Mill, Congleton Road,
   Nether Alderley, Macclesfield SK10
   4TW. Telephone: 01625 445853.
   Website: www.nationaltrust.org.uk
Quarry Bank Mill, Styal, Wilmslow SK9
   4LA. Telephone: 01625 445896.
   Website: www.nationaltrust.org.uk
Stretton Mill, Mill Lane, Stretton, near
   Farndon SY14 7RS.
   Telephone: 01606 41331.
   Website: www.strettonwatermill.org.uk

Cornwall
Cotehele Mill, St Dominick, Saltash.
   Telephone: 01579 350606.
   Website: www.nationaltrust.org.uk
Melinsey Mill, Veryan, Truro.
   Telephone: 01872 501049.

Lode Mill, on the National Trust's Anglesey Abbey estate in Cambridgeshire.

Trewey Mill and Wayside Folk Museum, Zennor, St Ives TR26 3DA.
Telephone: 01736 796945.
Wheal Martyn, Carthew, St Austell PL26 8XG.
Telephone: 01726 850362. Website: www.wheal-martyn.com

Cumbria
Acorn Bank Mill, Temple Sowerby, Penrith CA10 1SP.
Telephone: 01768 361893.
Website: www.nationaltrust.org.uk
Eskdale Mill, Boot, Holmrook CA19 1TG.
Telephone: 01946 723335.
Website: www.visitcumbria.com
Gleaston Mill, Gleaston, Ulverston LA12 0QH.
Telephone: 01229 869244.
Website: www.watermill.co.uk
Heron Corn Mill, Mill Lane, Beetham, Milnthorpe
LA7 7PQ. Telephone: 01539 565027.
Website: www.heronmill.org
Stott Park Bobbin Mill, Low Stott Park, Finsthwaite,
Ulverston. Telephone: 01539 531087.
Website: www.english-heritage.org.uk
The Watermill, Little Salkeld, Langwathby, Penrith
CA10 1NN. Telephone: 01768 881523.
Website: www.organicmill.co.uk

The drive to the millstones and the sack hoist in the Watermill at Little Salkeld, Cumbria.

Derbyshire
Arkwright's Cotton Mill, Mill Lane, Cromford,
Matlock DE24 3RQ. Telephone: 01629 823256.
Website: www.arkwrightsociety.org.uk
Caudwell's Mill, Rowsley DE4 2EB.
Telephone: 01629 734374.
Website: www.caudwellscrafts.co.uk
Stainsby Mill, Hardwick Hall, Doe Lea, Chesterfield S44 5QJ.
Telephone: 01246 850430. Website: www.nationaltrust.org.uk

Devon
Clyston Mill, Broadclyst, Exeter EX5 3EW.
Telephone: 01392 462425. Website: www.nationaltrust.org.uk
Coldharbour Mill, Uffculme, Cullompton EX15 3EE.
Telephone: 01884 840960. Website: www.coldharbourmill.org.uk
Finch Foundry and Museum, Sticklepath, Okehampton EX20 2NW.
Telephone: 01837 840046. Website: www.nationaltrust.org.uk
Manor Mill, Branscombe, Seaton EX12 3DB.
Telephone: 01392 881691. Website: www.nationaltrust.org.uk
Morwellham Quay, Tavistock PL19 8JL.
Telephone: 01822 832766. Website: www.morwellham-quay.co.uk
Otterton Mill, Otterton, Budleigh Salterton EX9 7HG.
Telephone: 01395 568521. Website: www.ottertonmill.com

Dorset
Castleton Water Wheel Museum, Oborne Road, Sherborne.
Telephone: 01935 813384. Website: www.castletonwaterwheelmuseum.org.uk
Mangerton Mill, Mangerton, Bridport DT6 3SG. Telephone: 01308 485224.
Sturminster Newton Mill, Sturminster Newton. Telephone: 01747 854355.
Website: www.sturminsternewton-museum.co.uk
The Town Mill, Mill Lane, Lyme Regis DT7 3PU.
Telephone: 01297 443579. Website: www.townmill.org.uk

White Mill, Sturminster Marshall, near Wimborne BH21 4BX.
Telephone: 01258 858051. Website: www.nationaltrust.org.uk, also www.whitemill.org

County Durham
Killhope, North of England Lead Mining Museum, near Cowshill, Upper Weardale DL13 1AR.
Telephone: 01388 537505. Website: www.killhope.org.uk
Path Head Mill, Summerhill, Blaydon, Gateshead NE21 4SP.
Telephone: 0191 414 6288. Website: www.gatesheadmill.co.uk

Essex
Bourne Mill, Bourne Road, Colchester CO2 8RT.
Telephone: 01206 572422. Website: www.nationaltrust.org.uk
Thorrington Mill, Thorrington, Brightlingsea.
Telephone: 01245 437663 or 07887 662177. Website: www.essexcc.gov.uk

Hampshire
Alderholt Mill, Fordingbridge SP6 1PU.
Telephone: 01425 653130. Website: www.alderholtmill.co.uk
City Mill, Bridge Street, Winchester SO23 8EJ.
Telephone: 01962 870057. Website: www.nationaltrust.org.uk
Eling Tide Mill, The Tollbridge, Totton, Southampton SO40 9HF. Telephone: 023 8086 9575.
Whitchurch Silk Mill, Winchester Street, Whitchurch RG28 7AL.
Telephone: 01256 892065. Website: www.whitchurchsilkmill.org.uk

Herefordshire
Mortimer's Cross Mill, Lucton, Leominster HR6 9PE. Telephone: 01568 708820.

Hertfordshire
Mill Green Mill, Hatfield AL9 5PD.
Telephone: 01707 271362. Website: www.hertsmuseums.org.uk
Redbournbury Mill, Redbournbury Lane, Redbourn Road, Redbourn, St Albans AL3 6RS.
Telephone: 01582 792874.
Website: www.redbournmill.co.uk

Isle of Wight
Calbourne Watermill and Museum, Newport Road,
Calbourne PO30 4JN. Telephone: 01983 531227.
Website: www.calbournewatermill.co.uk

Kent
Chart Gunpowder Mills, Westbrook Walk, Faversham.
Telephone: 01795 534542.
Website: www.faversham.org
Crabble Mill, Lower Road, River, Dover CT17 0UY.
Telephone: 08701 453857.
Website: www.ccmt.org.uk

Lancashire
Higher Mill, Holcombe Road, Helmshore, Rossendale
BB4 4NP. Telephone: 01706 226459.
Website: www.lancashire.gov.uk

*The overshot waterwheel at Redbournbury Mill,
Hertfordshire.*

Crabble Mill, Dover, Kent, an impressive brick and timber-framed building dating from 1812.

Lincolnshire
Cogglesford Mill, Sleaford.
Telephone: 01529 414294.
Website: www.lincolnshire.gov.uk

London
House Mill, Three Mills, Bromley by Bow.
Telephone: 020 8980 4626.
Website: www.housemill.org.uk

Norfolk
Gunton Park Sawmill, White Post Lane,
Gunton Park NR11 7HL.
Telephone: 01603 222705.
Website: www.norfolkmills.co.uk/watermills
Letheringsett Mill, Riverside Road,
Letheringsett, Holt.
Telephone: 01263 713153.
Website: www.letheringsettwatermill.co.uk

Northumberland
Heatherslaw Mill, Ford, Cornhill-on-Tweed TD12 4TJ.
Telephone: 01890 820338. Website: www.ford-and-etal.co.uk

Nottinghamshire
Ollerton Mill, Ollerton. Telephone: 01623 822469. Website: www.nottinghamshire.gov.uk

Oxfordshire
Coleshill Mill, Coleshill, Swindon SN6 7PT.
Telephone: 01793 762209. Website: www.nationaltrust.org.uk

The upstream face of Alvingham Mill, on the River Lud, in Lincolnshire.

Mapledurham Mill, the last working watermill on the River Thames.

Mapledurham Mill, Mapledurham, Reading RG4 7TR.
Telephone: 0118 972 3350. Website: www.mapledurham.co.uk

Shropshire
Daniel's Mill, Eardington, Bridgnorth WV16 5JL.
Telephone: 01746 762753. Website: www.shropshiretourism.info

Somerset
Bishop's Lydeard Mill, Mill Lane, Bishop's Lydeard, Taunton TA4 3LN.
Telephone: 01823 432151. Website: www.bishopslydeardmill.co.uk
Burcott Mill, Burcott, Wookey, Wells BA5 1NJ.
Telephone: 01749 673118. Website: www.burcottmill.com
Claverton Pumping Station, Ferry Lane, Claverton, Bath BA2 7BH.
Telephone: 01225 483001. Website: www.claverton.org
Dunster Mill, Mill Lane, Dunster TA24 6SW.
Telephone: 01643 821759. Website: www.nationaltrust.org.uk
Gant's Mill, Bruton BA10 0DB. Telephone: 01749 812393. Website: www.gantsmill.co.uk
Saltford Brass Mill, Saltford, Bristol. Telephone: 01225 872954. Website: www.brassmill.com
Wookey Hole Paper Mill, Wookey, Wells BA5 1BB.
Telephone: 01749 672243. Website: www.wookey.co.uk

Staffordshire
Brindley's Mill, Mill Street, Leek ST13 8HA.
Telephone: 01538 483741. Website: www.brindleymill.net
Cheddleton Flint Mill, Cheddleton, Leek ST13 5HL.
Telephone: 0161 408 5083. Website: www.people.ex.ac.uk/akoutram/cheddleton-mill
Mosty Lea Mill, Stone ST15 8TD. Telephone: 01785 813407. Website: www.kibblestone.org
Shugborough Estate Mill, Shugborough, Stafford ST17 0XB.
Telephone: 01889 881388. Website: www.shugborough.org.uk

The mill house and early-nineteenth-century watermill at Pakenham, Suffolk.

Suffolk
Alton Mill, Museum of East Anglian Life, Stowmarket IP14 1DL.
 Telephone: 01449 612229. Website: www.eastanglianlife.org.uk
Pakenham Mill, Grimstone End, Pakenham IP31 2ND.
 Telephone: 01787 230269. Website: www.pakenhamwatermill.co.uk
Woodbridge Tide Mill, Woodbridge. Telephone: 01473 626618. Website: www.tidemill.org.uk

Surrey
Cobham Mill, High Street, Cobham.
 Telephone: 01932 867387. Website: www.cobhamheritage.org.uk/cobhammill
Shalford Mill, Shalford, Guildford GU4 8BS.
 Telephone: 01483 561389. Website: www.nationaltrust.org.uk

The restored and preserved tide mill at Woodbridge, Suffolk.

Charlecote Mill,
Hampton Lucy,
Warwickshire.

Sussex, East
Michelham Priory Mill, Upper Dicker, near Hailsham BN27 3QS.
Telephone: 01323 844224. Website: www.sussexpast.co.uk
Park Mill, Bateman's, Burwash, Etchingham TN19 7DS.
Telephone: 01435 882302. Website: www.nationaltrust.org.uk

Sussex, West
Coultershaw Beam Pump, Petworth.
Telephone: 01798 865774. Website: www.coultershaw.co.uk
Lurgashall Mill, Weald & Downland Open Air Museum, Singleton PO18 0EU.
Telephone: 01243 811363. Website: www.wealddown.co.uk

Warwickshire
Charlecote Mill, Hampton Lucy, Stratford-upon-Avon CV35 8BB.
Telephone: 01789 842072. Website: www.charlecotemill.co.uk
New Hall Mill, Wylde Green Road, Sutton Coldfield B76 1QU.
Telephone: 0121 526 3131. Website: www.newhallmill.org.uk
Sarehole Mill, Cole Bank Road, Hall Green, Birmingham B13 0BD.
Telephone: 0121 777 6612. Website: www.bmag.org.uk

Worcestershire
Churchill Forge, Churchill, Kidderminster DY10 3LX.
Telephone: 01562 700476. Website: www.churchillforge.org.uk
Forge Mill Needle Museum, Needle Mill Lane, Riverside, Redditch B98 8HY.
Telephone: 01527 62509. Website: www.forgemill.org.uk

Yorkshire, North
Fountains Abbey Mill, Fountains Abbey and Studley Royal Estate, Ripon HG4 3DY.
Telephone: 01765 608888. Website: www.fountainsabbey.org.uk
Raindale Mill, Castle Museum, York.
Telephone: 01904 687687. Website: www.yorkcastlemuseum.org.uk
Tockett's Mill, Skelton Road, Guisborough TS14 6QA.
Telephone: 01287 634437. Website: www.redcar-cleveland.gov.uk

Yorkshire, South
Abbeydale Industrial Hamlet and Shepherd Wheel, Abbeydale Road South, Sheffield S7 2QW.
Telephone: 0114 236 7731. Website: www.simt.co.uk
Top Forge, Forge Lane, Thurgoland, near Barnsley S35 7DN.
Telephone: 0114 288 7576. Website: www.topforge.co.uk
Worsbrough Mill Museum, Worsbrough Bridge, Worsbrough, Barnsley S70 5LJ.
Telephone: 01226 774527. Website: www.barnsley.gov.uk/tourism

Yorkshire, West
Leeds Industrial Museum, Armley Mills, Canal Road, Armley, Leeds LS12 2QF.
Telephone: 0113 263 7861. Website: www.leeds.gov.uk/armleymills
Thwaite Mills, Great Lane, Stourton, Leeds LS10 1RP.
Telephone: 0113 276 2887. Website: www.leeds.gov.uk/thwaitemills

Channel Islands
Quetivel Mill, St Peter's Valley, Jersey.
Telephone: 01534 483193. Website: www.nationaltrustjersey.org.je

Isle of Man
Lady Isabella Waterwheel, Laxey. Telephone: 01624 648000. Website: www.gov.im/mnh

Scotland
Barony Mills, Birsay, Orkney KW17 2LY.
Telephone: 01856 721439. Website: www.birsay.org.uk/baronymill.htm
Barry Mill, Barry, Carnoustie, Angus DD7 7RJ.
Telephone: 01241 856761. Website: www.nts.org.uk
Blair Atholl Mill, Blair Atholl, Pitlochry, Perthshire PH18 5SH.
Telephone: 01796 481321. Website: www.blairathollwatermill.co.uk
Click Mill, Dounby, Orkney.
Telephone: 01856 841815. Website: www.historic-scotland.gov.uk
Crofthouse Museum, South Voe, Dunrossness, Shetland.
Telephone: 01595 695057. Website: www.shetlandheritageassociation.com
New Abbey Corn Mill, New Abbey, Dumfries.
Telephone: 01387 850260. Website: www.historic-scotland.gov.uk
Preston Mill, East Linton, East Lothian EH40 3DS.
Telephone: 01620 860426. Website: www.nts.org.uk
Quendale Mill, Dunrossness, South Mainland, Shetland ZE2 9JD.
Telephone: 01950 460405 or 460465. Website: www.quendalemill.shetland.co.uk
Siabost Mill, Siabost, Lewis, Western Isles. Telephone: 01851 710208.

Wales
Bacheldre Mill, Church Stoke, Montgomery, Powys SY15 6TE.
Telephone: 01588 620489. Website: www.bacheldremill.co.uk
Carew Tidal Mill, Carew, Tenby, Pembrokeshire SA70 8SL.
Telephone: 01646 651782. Website: www.carewcastle.com
Y Felin, Mill Street, St Dogmaels, Cardigan SA43 3DY.
Telephone: 01239 613999. Website: www.yfelin.co.uk
Y Felin Dolws, Gower Heritage Centre, Parkmill, Swansea.
Telephone: 01792 371206. Website: www.gowerheritagecentre.co.uk
Gelligroes Mill, Pontllanfraith, Caerphilly.
Telephone: 01495 222322. Website: www.caerphilly.gov.uk
Llywernog Silver Lead Mine Museum, Ponterwyd, Aberystwyth, Ceredigion SY23 3AB.
Telephone: 01970 890620. Website: www.silverminetours.co.uk

Wellbrook Beetling Mill, Corkhill, County Tyrone. Here a breastshot waterwheel drives seven beetling engines, used to beat a sheet into linen cloth, the final process in its manufacture.

Melin Howell, Llanddeusant, Anglesey. Telephone: 01407 730240.
Museum of Welsh Life, St Fagans, Cardiff CF5 6XB.
   Telephone: 029 2057 3500. Website: www.museumwales.ac.uk
National Woollen Museum, Drefach Felindre, Newcastle Emlyn, Carmarthenshire SA44 5UP.
   Telephone: 01559 370929. Website: www.museumwales.ac.uk
Rock Mill, Capel Dewi, Llandysul, Ceredigion SA44 4PH.
   Telephone: 01559 362356. Website: www.rockmillwales.co.uk
Welsh Slate Museum, Padarn Country Park, Llanberis, Gwynedd LL55 4TY.
   Telephone: 01286 870630. Website: www.museumwales.ac.uk

Northern Ireland
Annalong Mill, Annalong, County Down. Telephone: 028 4175 2256.
Castle Ward Mills, Strangford, County Down BT30 7LS.
   Telephone: 028 4488 1204. Website: www.nationaltrust.org.uk
Florence Court Sawmill, Florence Court, near Enniskillen, County Fermanagh BT92 1DB.
   Telephone: 028 6634 8249. Website: www.nationaltrust.org.uk
Ulster Folk and Transport Museum, Cultra, Holywood, County Down BT18 0EU.
   Telephone: 028 9042 8428. Website: www.uftm.org.uk
Wellbrook Beetling Mill, Corkhill, Cookstown, County Tyrone BT80 9RY.
   Telephone: 028 8674 8210. Website: www.nationaltrust.org.uk

Index

Page numbers in italic refer to illustrations